The Ten Million Dollar Employee

*When Your Most Toxic Liability Meets
Your Most Important Customer*

By Steven L. Blue

The Ten Million Dollar Employee

When Your Most Toxic Liability Meets Your Most Important Customer

By Steven L. Blue

The Ten Million Dollar Employee: When Your Most Toxic Liability Meets Your Most Important Customer

ISBN: 978-0-9822589-0-3

Library of Congress Catalogue Number: 2010941917

For more information or to purchase additional copies contact:

Steven L. Blue

www.stevebluewebsite.com

steve@stevebluewebsite.com

Super Ceo Press

507-474-4734

78 Shady Oak Ct.

Winona, MN 55987

About The Author

Steve is a Super CEO, author, and keynote speaker. He has vast experience in transforming sleepy little businesses into global goliaths. In one case, he increased margins by over 60%. In another, he tripled profits using his Pay As You Grow ^{SM} system, which means growing earnings without the need for outside capital while maintaining dividends.

Steve has 19 years experience in markets all over the world. In that time he has formed very successful international ventures and transformed businesses with no international presence into global powerhouses. In one case, he increased a company's international sales from 0 to 24% of total sales.

Steve spent 7 years in a turnaround where the organization had to make choices between paying employees or the utility bill. That is where he developed his skills in strict operational control and cash management. While he was there the company returned to profitability, and along the way he transformed the worst performing division to the best in less than 2 years.

Steve started his career as a factory supervisor and quickly became known as the "go to" problem-solving guy. He would routinely fix under-performing departments, which is where he gained a deep knowledge of most functional areas of a company. And in every assignment he substantially increased productivity and reduced cost. He has worked in industries as diverse as publishing and industrial automation.

In 32 years in management, the last 15 as a P&L executive, Steve has solved problems you can't imagine. And he has never failed to deliver double digit gains in anything he's touched.

That is why he is completely confident when he says you don't have a problem he hasn't already seen. In fact, you don't have a problem he hasn't already solved. And you don't have a business that can't triple its profits.

Steve has a BS Degree from the State University of New York and an MBA from Regis University.

For more information about Steve go to www.stevebluewebsite.com

Introduction

Imagine this. You just acquired one of your competitors. It was a deal made in heaven because it doubled the size of your company and gave you market access and technical capability that rounds out your portfolio. Even better, you are now in a position to dominate your market space.

The facilities you acquired are nothing less than spectacular. The main entrance features a dramatic foyer with an enormous cascading waterfall. The offices are all mahogany and smoked glass. Rare artwork and marble everywhere. What a grand statement this would make with your most important customers!

So you decide to have an open house and show it to them. But there is just one problem. Somehow, one of the buildings in this marvelous, marble campus slipped past your due diligence team.

This building is an Environmental Protection Agency dream—and your nightmare. I mean, this building is nasty. Toxic sludge all over the place. Old drums with chemicals oozing out of them. The place reeks of sodium chloride. Asbestos everywhere. Sewers that haven't been cleaned in decades. Toilets plugged up for years. You can't even stand to walk in the place without feeling the urge to vomit. This building is your most toxic liability.

So now you have a choice. As you take your most important customers for a tour of your nice new campus—

are you going to bring them into that toxic wasteland? Are you going to introduce your most important customer to your most toxic liability? Of course not—only an idiot would do that.

And if you did, what do you suppose the consequences would be? You know the answer to that—goodbye customer.

So what do you do if your most important customer wanders into that building? Gee I am sorry Mr. Customer; I'll speak to the building and ask it to be nicer next time? Gee, I am sorry Mr. Customer; I'll put the building in a 12-step improvement program so it won't be so nasty the next time you meet it? Gee, I am sorry Mr. Customer; I'll try and clean it up a bit before the next time you visit? Of course not—only an idiot would do that.

Well guess what? This is happening right now in your company. Every day, your most toxic liabilities meet your most important customers. But these liabilities are not buildings. They are your Ten Million Dollar toxic employee liabilities. And you lose business with every encounter between them and your most important customers. Every single encounter.

And how do I know you have toxic employees? Because I encounter them every day. In all kinds of businesses. And when I encounter them I make decisions that imperil the future of these companies. And so do your customers.

So what are you doing about these toxic employees? I'll bet you have your human resource people ask them to be nicer next time. Or maybe you put them in a 12-step self-improvement or sensitivity training program. Or maybe you give them a warning to clean up their act.

And what you should be doing is getting rid of them—all of them. You need to clean up your "employee balance sheet". Every day, your employee balance sheet is weakening your financial balance sheet with every encounter your most toxic employees have with your most important customers.

But there is another side to your employee balance sheet. The side that has your most important human assets. The side that has your Ten Million Dollar golden asset employees. This is the side you should be strengthening.

You see, your company has all Ten Million Dollar Employees. The question you have to ask yourself is this: Are they Ten Million Dollar liabilities or Ten Million Dollar assets? The answer to that question determines whether your company is on a trajectory to triple its profits or tumble into oblivion.

The key to tripling profits in your company is by restructuring your employee balance sheet to eliminate your toxic employees and make heroes out of your Ten Million Dollar golden asset employees.

Know this: You have them. They have infiltrated your company. They are wrecking your company as you read this. And as the CEO, you have allowed this condition to exist. You have allowed your human resource people to bamboozle you into tolerating 12-step sensitivity training programs. You have allowed your union negotiations to produce agreements that tolerate toxic employees (some would argue union agreements promote toxic employees). You, Mr. CEO, have allowed this to happen to your company. And only you, Mr. CEO, can fix it. This book will show you how—if you have the guts to do it.

Praise for The Ten Million Dollar Employee

A quick read with a big message. Steve drives home the fact that as CEOs we must understand that our employees are the windows to our company. After reading this, it is critical that we identify our toxic employees and get rid of them. At the same time, we need to reap, recognize, and reward our $10 million dollar people.

Tom Wynn
President & CEO
Peerless Chain Company

Steve Blue has it right. Beautiful spaces are nice but if the people in those places don't treat us well, we focus on that experience and not on the gleaming space. It pays to remember that as far as our visitors and customers are concerned, every employee *IS* the organization. The corollary to this is that as leaders we must treat our own staff well. It is hard, if not impossible, to recover some gold from a thoroughly toxic person—better to avoid creating toxic people in the first place.

Judith A. Ramaley
President
Winona State University

Everything you always knew and sometimes forget to practice describes the lessons or reminders in this book. A must read for all who care about how their company takes care of their customers.

Tom Severson
President & CEO
Severson Oil Company

If your organic growth is not what you want it to be, or your customer service appears to work near a revolving door, then this is the book for you. In The *$10 Million Dollar Employee*, Super CEO Steve Blue makes a strong case through straight talking examples and the top 5 reasons these toxic employees exist in your organization. This book will bring the problem into focus and move you to take action. No organization can afford to ignore this age-old problem and Steve Blue gives you the tools to fix it, now.

Craig W. Porter
General Manager
PlastiCert, Inc.

With elegant clarity, Steven Blue reveals the formula for growing the corporate balance sheet…grow the *employee* balance sheet! Grow the golden assets and fire the toxic liabilities with haste. Million$ are at stake.

Bud Baechler
Business Advisor and former CEO
Mediawerks

Steven gives you "no-nonsense" advice that, when applied, will virtually guarantee business success. Everyone has encountered both great and lousy employees, but Steven removes all doubt about the total impact on the bottom line of each type. This book is engaging, fun to read, and packed with wisdom.

Peter A. Land, MS, CSP, CMC, CPCM

In his usual direct (dare I say, blunt) style, Steve Blue tackles one of the most critical aspects of running a company—human capital. Although he uses many examples of human capital from his vast array of experiences, the fundamental and serious point remains the same in the book. And it is that the balance sheet of human capital, looked at as assets and liabilities, is just as important as the financial balance sheets that executives may be using. The difference of course, as Steve Blue shows, is that rather than a balance of human capital assets and liabilities, a company had better weigh its human capital heavily towards assets if it is to survive in this very competitive global environment.

Gabriel Manrique
Globalization Specialist
Fastenal Company

Steven Blue's *The $10 Million Dollar Employee* imparts with great clarity and passion the principles that underlie success in life—truth, respect, accountability and commitment. Through a series of personal narratives and anecdotes, Mr. Blue substantively entertains and inspires the reader to think creatively and act deliberatively. It is a compelling road map for leaders in all walks of life.

Dave Gudmastad
Director of Bands
Cotter High School

The $10 Million Dollar Employee is an entertaining read with a very serious business message woven throughout the story. You will benefit from Super CEO Steve L Blue's good business sense, and just good sense. His advice on "toxic employees" and "golden assets" will be helpful to any organization with employees. You will find yourself nodding in agreement as you turn each page.

Robert J. Schrupp
President/Founder
Therapy Network, Inc

Through Steve's entertaining, vivid and realistic stories, he has captured the importance of a CEO to recognize their responsibility in assuring a culture of "ultimate service to the customer" while not allowing this culture to be undermined by a single employee. Leaders in business must realize how destructive just one "toxic" employee can be and must react to this toxicity by eliminating it no matter how difficult it will be. Toxic behavior spreads and eats away at the foundation of a business all the while building an army of disgruntled and former customers which will destroy a business's bottom line if left unattended. A leader must take charge by eliminating a toxic employee and embrace the $10 million dollar employee and all that he/she represents to your organization. It is imperative in the dynamic global workplace we live in today.

James Johnson
President
Minnesota State College Southeast Technical

Table of Contents

Chapter 1: The Destruction of a $10 Million Hotel

A while back, my family and I stayed at a brand-spanking new hotel. I walked into the lobby and it had crystal chandeliers and marble everywhere. There was oak and cherry trim. The outside of the building was constructed with tuckpoint and brick, and it had an expensive and perfectly manicured lawn and landscaping. The fitness center was fabulous, and there were moist chocolate chip cookies at the front desk.

This hotel had the "wow" factor as soon as you walked in the door; it was very impressive. I figured they had to spend $10 million on this hotel if they spent a dime. That very night, one employee nearly destroyed that $10 million investment, while another saved it. We checked in very late. My kids were very young then, and they were cranky from the trip, not to mention hungry, so we called room service. It rang and rang and rang. My kids were getting crankier, and my wife was none too happy either. Of course, they were looking to their CEO dad to make something happen.

I decided to go down to the restaurant to get something to bring back to the room. It was just my luck that I shared the elevator with a restaurant/room service employee. The problem was, she was crankier than my kids! She had a room service order in her hands and I thought this was the perfect chance to solve my problem. I asked her how it was going, and she said, "Terrible! Can you believe that not only do I have to cook the room service food, but I have to deliver it, too? I hate this place. I hate this job."

At that point, I figured she hated me, too, but I decided to continue. "Why are you working all alone?" She said she had no idea, but figured her boss was just trying to save money. She hated him, too. I asked her if I could get a room service order, and she said, "Fat chance."

Think about this. That hotel spent $10 million on this place, and they're trying to save a few pesos in restaurant help! What's worse, they are letting their most toxic liability meet their most lucrative revenue source: me, a CEO and world traveler. Does that make sense? Do you think this happens in your business? I'd bet it does. Unfortunately, my story gets worse.

I had to go back to the room and explain to my kids why their big-shot CEO dad couldn't get them any food; I'd rather face an angry customer any day. However, that wasn't the end of my problems that night.

It was past 11 o'clock, and we decided we might as well tuck the kids in bed. However, we discovered that the hide-a-bed had no sheets or blankets. Imagine trying to get something from housekeeping at that time of night! By this time, I am convinced that I will never stay at this hotel again, period. How much am I worth over my lifetime as a world traveler? How much revenue will that hotel lose because they spent all their money on a $10 million building and nothing on servicing their customers? How many other high value customers did this angry employee reach that night? How many high value customers did she reach in a week? A month? A year? What's that lost revenue worth? The short answer is a boatload.

However, let's get back to my story. I am a super CEO, so I am going to make something happen, dammit! I called the front desk, fully expecting a, "Sorry, nobody on from housekeeping at this time of night," but what I got was a completely different answer. The front desk guy profusely apologized for the inconvenience and promised sheets and blankets in five minutes. *Yeah, right*. How many times have you heard a promise from the front desk of a hotel that was ignored?

Sure enough, less than five minutes later, the front desk guy *himself* was at my door. He had a big smile on his face, and plenty of sheets and blankets! He went to the housekeeping area and got them himself. He apologized again for the inconvenience and promised to alert the manager the next morning. It was because of the front desk employee that I decided to give that hotel another chance to earn my future business. The restaurant employee nearly wrecked this hotel's $10 million investment, while the same night, the front desk employee saved it.

I had two very different experiences that night from two very different employees. Both worked for the same company. Both worked for the same hotel manager. Both were probably paid comparable wages. Both are $10 million employees, but the restaurant employee is a $10 million toxic liability. The front desk employee is a $10 million asset.

Why is that? How can two employees, under similar conditions, behave so differently? Think about how many times have you been on an airplane and encountered a flight

The Destruction of a $10 Million Hotel

attendant with a bad attitude (OK, trick question, that is most of them), and on the same flight then encountered a flight attendant with a great attitude? How can this be? They make about the same money. They have the same job, work for the same company, and probably for the same supervisor.

Where is the supervisor in all of this? I know what you are thinking: The supervisor couldn't possibly know which employee is the liability and which is the asset. Do you really believe that? Do you really believe every supervisor on the planet doesn't know which employees are gold and which ones are junk? Of course they do.

You see, every business has $10 million employees. Your business is loaded with $10M employees. In fact, every single one of your employees is a $10M employee, but some are assets, and some are liabilities, *toxic liabilities*. All of your employees fall into one category or another. Just like your balance sheet, there is no middle ground. What happens to your company if it has more liabilities than assets? It's the same thing with your employee balance sheet.

There is a battle going on every day in your company, a battle between your greatest assets and your most toxic liabilities. It is fought by your $10M employees. If you're still in business, it is only because of your $10M asset employees. Every day they undo (you hope) the damage done by your $10M toxic liability employees. The battle is fought for your most lucrative sources of revenue and the fate of your business. Make no mistake, this goes on every single day in your business, and you don't even know it.

However, your customers do. They make decisions about the future of your business based on encounters with

The Ten Million Dollar Employee

your $10M employees. The equation is simple: If your customers have more encounters with your $10M toxic liability employees than your $10M asset employees, your business is toast. You'll probably blame the market, the competition, or the economy, when the answer is so much simpler.

Who will win this battle? Your $10M asset employees or your $10M liability employees? The answer to that determines the fate of your company. The logic is simple. If you have even one $10M toxic liability employee, you risk much. Certainly, if you have more $10M toxic liability employees than $10M asset employees, you lose, especially if your toxic liabilities face your most lucrative sources of revenue every day.

Think about this: When my family walked into the hotel that night, what did they care about? Did they care that the chandeliers were crystal? Did they care about the finely manicured lawn? Did they care about the fabulous fitness center? Of course not. What they cared about was getting to the room, grabbing a bite to eat and going to bed. All the hard assets in the world can't make that happen, but people can.

Did that hotel have to spend $10M to give the average family what they cared about most that night? Of course not, but a $10M employee can. Service businesses are notorious for matching their most toxic liabilities with their most important customers. Airlines put the most senior flight attendants on international flights to attend to their most important customers, first/business class customers. Mind you, they don't put their most important assets on those flights. They put their $10M toxic liability employees on

The Destruction of a $10 Million Hotel

those flights because of seniority, matching them up with the guys who pay the most for a ticket. I don't want to hear that they have no choice because of their union agreements. It takes two parties to make an agreement; you can't blame the union for something to which management agreed.

The mistake service businesses make is simple: They plough all their dough in hard assets, like buildings and aircraft. They think the solution to retaining customers is to have the slickest buildings and sleekest aircrafts. They only look at the balance sheet. Yeah, let's spend $10M on marble and 180-degree reclining aircraft seats, and then put those assets in the hands of our most toxic liabilities. That makes a lot of sense. Is my dripping sarcasm pervading these pages? I hope so. Service employees are almost an afterthought, a necessary evil. The service industry thinks employees won't matter if you have a lot of marble in the building or a Bose headset in first class.

Airlines have it all wrong. They think the code-sharing agreements, landing rights, fuel efficiency of the aircrafts, and the pilots are the most important parts of the equation; they're not. Airline customers could care less about any of those things. Most of them never see or hear from the pilot. I bring my own headsets, and I can't sleep on a plane no matter what kind of seat is provided. What most airline customers care about is how they are treated on the plane. The most important part of the equation is the flight attendant. More importantly, the most important flight attendant is the one that encounters their highest value customers in first class and business class.

The Ten Million Dollar Employee

Hotels have it all wrong. They think wifi, fitness centers, and award-winning restaurants are the most important part of the equation; they're not. Most hotel customers don't even use the restaurant. Many hotel customers have an iPhone or a Blackberry, and don't even use the wifi. They could care less about marble floors. What they care about is how they are treated by all those $10M employees running around the hotel. The most important part of the hotel equation is the employee at the front desk; that is the person hotel customers look to when they need something.

Now, I travel a lot. I've had a lot of encounters with $10M employees, and I've experienced the difference it can make. I decide the fate of these businesses every day based upon those encounters, and it's not just the service industry that I observe and judge every day. I have a keen eye for the $10M employees in the supermarket, at the local pizza delivery company, where I receive my medical care, and where I buy my car. I decide the fate of these companies every single day. Every day, people are deciding the fate of your company, just like I do.

Don't think that just because you may not be in the service industry that you don't have this problem. The battle between toxic liabilities and your $10M heroes happens in every industry, every day. You see, your customers probably aren't going to tell you that you have too many toxic liability employees. They probably don't even know that's the problem. They won't stop to think about it as I do. They will simply switch their business to a company that has more $10M asset employees than you do. You won't know it until they are gone, and you won't even know why.

The Destruction of a $10 Million Hotel

You don't need to go to business school to learn the best and worst practices in business. All you have to do is observe the world around you, and take those observations back to your business to make it better. That is what I do every day, and that is the purpose of this book: to give you a glimpse into what I see every day, the best and the worst in the $10M employee. Do as I have done. Ask yourself the hard questions: Is what I saw today happening in my business? Do I have an all-star team of $10M asset employees, or a bunch of dud $10M toxic liability employees? Once you know the answer to that second question, your path is clear and simple...but not easy. Don't blame the competition. Don't blame the economy. Don't blame the outside world. Don't place fault somewhere else. You're the CEO; you're at fault. You're the CEO; you alone have the power to fix it. You're the CEO; you're in charge...except when you're not.

Always remember this: You are not the CEO—Edith is.

Chapter 2: You Are Not the CEO—Edith Is

My family and I had been planning a vacation for nearly a year. My children were in their teens, so family vacations were hard to coordinate around everyone's schedules. The time that we could spend together was important to me, so every detail was mapped out carefully.

The first part of our week together was spent on our boat, cruising up the Mississippi River. We spent the first several nights sleeping on the boat in different ports. We finally had come to the place where everyone was looking forward to a hot shower and room service at a nice hotel.

This was an annual trip, so we had been to this hotel before. It offered a welcome respite from the close quarters of our boat. Everyone was hot, tired, and cranky from spending several days cooped up boating on the river. Everyone was anxious to get checked in and spread out.

I had arranged for the rooms eight months before our arrival. I clearly specified that I needed two non-smoking adjoining rooms. My confirmation notice stated as such. I called the hotel a few weeks before just to double-check. They assured me that yes, everything was set.

With confirmation in hand and my hot, tired, and hungry family in tow, I stepped up to the check-in counter, anxious to get checked in and to our rooms. The first person that greeted me that day was the hotel's most toxic liability—Edith.

You Are Not the CEO—Edith Is

When you check into a hotel, the most important person in your world is the front desk employee. They have the power to make you delighted or miserable. They shape your opinions right from the start as to whether this is a good place to stay or not. They are the face of the hotel. They have all the power in the world, and you have none.

If you're like most people, you will make a decision about staying there again in the first 10 seconds of your encounter with the front desk employee. The front desk employee doesn't make decisions about hard assets. They don't make decisions about marble and manicured lawns. However, the front desk employee does make most of the decisions that your customers care about, and they do this in less than two minutes. In less than two minutes, the front desk employee determines the fate of the hotel—forever. Sounds like the job of the CEO, doesn't it? However, at that moment, you are not the CEO—Edith is.

Edith was a grumpy old gal. She'd had a hard life, and it showed. Her voice was raspy from smoking too much, and she looked like life had just passed her by. All those disappointments in her life had taken their toll. She dreamed of traveling the world someday and then tending to her pool in Florida. She never expected to end up a measly, lowly, front desk clerk. She was the queen of the prom in high school, and now she was the queen of the front desk? Life was such a disappointment!

People like Edith want to take out their disappointments on you. How people like Edith get in such high profile positions with customers is beyond me. Some hotel bonehead must have thought, "Hey, I have a great idea.

The Ten Million Dollar Employee

Let's take our employee who is most likely to offend the customer and put her in the most likely place she can do so: the front desk!"

Edith has a mindless routine that makes her difficult life easier. It gets her through the day without having to think very hard, or at all. She has better things to think about than how she does her job, like how soon she can pop open that beer and smoke that cigarette when she gets home! She doesn't see her role as welcoming people and making sure their first impression at the hotel is a delightful one. Edith is very clear about what her job is: Her job is to herd the cattle in, and get them in as fast as possible. When they are ready to leave, Edith is to herd the cattle out. Have you ever had this experience at a hotel? Edith is tired of suffering fools that step up to her front desk and ask for things that don't fit into her routine, suffering fools like me—the hotel's most lucrative source of revenue. Edith doesn't believe cattle should ask for or want anything. They should only want to be herded in and herded out.

As soon as I saw her, I knew I was in for trouble. I could tell by the way she looked at me this was not going to be a happy encounter, so I decided to tread carefully. After all, at that moment, Edith is the most important person in my world. At that moment, Edith has all the power, and I have none.

I cheerily said, "Good morning, Edith. How are you today?" She grunted something about a tired back and sore feet, and asked for my name. Uh oh, this is going to be worse than I thought. This tough old cookie already was shaping the destiny of her company. I already was deciding the future of the hotel, and I hadn't been there more than a minute.

She barked something off and handed me some keys. Gee, I'm sorry. I missed the, "Welcome to our hotel, Mr. Blue, nice to have you here," or anything remotely similar. I looked at the keys, and the room numbers didn't look as if they would be adjoining. I said, "Excuse me, Edith, I reserved two adjoining non-smoking rooms, is that what I have?"

Wouldn't you know, the rooms were smoking and on different floors. Smoking is bad enough, but if you have a 16-year-old daughter with you (who needs her own room, of course), the last thing you can accept is having her on a different floor. Now, I am a CEO, so I am used to getting things the way I want. If I could talk to the real CEO of the hotel, you can be sure I would get it. He would understand that I am his most lucrative source of revenue, and he would make it right. However, at this moment Edith is the CEO, and Edith is not happy.

Therefore, I said, "Excuse me, Edith, but I really need an adjoining room for my daughter, and smoking is not acceptable. I am really hoping you can help me out here." I even showed her my confirmation to prove it. However, that didn't matter to Edith, because her routine is to herd the cattle, and she wants the hotel's computer to automatically assign rooms, so she doesn't have to take on extra work.

She rolled her eyes and kind of sighed. Oh, life would be so much easier for Edith without customers. She reluctantly started hunting in the computer for the right rooms. It took about 45 seconds, and she finally came up with what I had reserved in the first place.

The Ten Million Dollar Employee

It was clear that I was a huge imposition on her mindless day. When she was done, I thanked her. She said, "Well, it was a lot of extra work, but I got it done." Forty-five seconds is a lot of extra work? What else did she have to do in the moment, anyway? I looked behind me, and there wasn't even anyone else in line!

In stark contrast to Edith's place is the Depot Hotel in Minneapolis. When you check in there, the front desk employee doesn't simply hand you your key; he walks around to your side of the front desk to present you with it, along with some helpful information about the hotel. He is not herding cattle in and out; he is welcoming an old friend back into his home. In the first 10 seconds of that encounter, I decided the fate of that company.

What is the difference between these two encounters? Both hotels had a front desk. Both hotels had a front desk employee. However, one had a toxic liability meeting its most lucrative source of income, and the other had a golden $10M asset employee meeting it. That is the difference. In less than two minutes, Edith destroyed the investment that the hotel had made in the future of its business. In less than two minutes, the Depot Hotel secured its future with me forever.

If you are a CEO, you probably already know that "command and control" from the executive suite is an illusion. If you think you're in control of very much, think again. Edith is in control, and she hates her job. Nice combination, eh? You might as well hand her your keys to the executive suite, because before long, you won't need them.

If you are a CEO, you probably already know that you are the person with the least amount of power over the fate of your company (or at least you should already know this). If you think you have the most amount of power over the fate of your company, think again. Edith has the most power over the fate of your company, and she could care less.

Edith has the power to destroy your company, and she's doing it. Not in a single transaction, or in a single day, but over time, day-by-day, Edith is destroying your company. So are all the other toxic liabilities just like her. If you are the CEO, you should be fired for allowing your most toxic liabilities to run amok in your company.

Now, you may argue that no one knows how toxic Edith is. Do you really believe that? *Someone* does. I'd bet her immediate supervisor knows it, certainly. If he doesn't know it, he should be fired. However, I am guessing he knows it and doesn't do anything, because he is a toxic liability, too.

On the other hand, you wouldn't be in business if you didn't have some offsetting golden employee assets. When they go to work, they make a different decision than Edith does. They decide to be golden $10M assets and give everything they can to their jobs. They decide to choose excellence over cattle herding. The problem is that those golden assets don't usually have the impact on your most important customers the way that Edith does. Your customers expect excellence, so often it is not remarkable when they get it. What they do not expect is to be treated poorly. Therefore, when they meet Edith, the impact is enormous, and it can take more than one golden asset employee to offset just one Edith.

That's what happened in my case. Edith made such a negative impact on me that it would have been nearly impossible for any amount of $10M asset employees to offset the damage that Edith did. Unfortunately, during our two-day stay there, I did not even encounter one! The last image in my mind from that hotel is, heaven forbid, Edith! In fact, Edith is the image in my mind whenever I think about that hotel. Is Edith the last and everlasting image you want your most important customers to have when thinking of your company?

Edith's hotel is guilty of double jeopardy. They have a bunch of toxic liabilities running around and no offsetting assets. It was almost as if the other employees weren't even there. It's not like they made a bad impression; they simply made *no* impression at all. If only the hotel had some $10M superheroes, it might have been able to save my business, but it didn't.

When your financial balance sheet has all liabilities and no offsetting assets, what happens to your company? The same thing that happens in your employee balance sheet. If you have a bunch of toxic liabilities running around (or in the case of this hotel, just one) and no offsetting $10M superheroes, you're headed for the scrap heap. Even simply having a few more $10M superheroes is not enough to win the battle against your most toxic assets. You cannot afford to have even one toxic liability because of the inordinate impact it has on your most important customers. I know you're sitting back right about now thinking that it is impossible for any business not to have a few toxic liabilities around. No, it is not impossible; I have done it. You should have to make the commitment to accept nothing less than the $10M superheroes, and then go to work on making that happen.

For the longest time, I thought no single employee ever could have the same impact on me that Edith had. For the longest time, I believed no single employee ever again could decide the fate of a company in the blink of an eye. However, I was soon to learn that I was wrong.

Chapter 3: You're Not Leaving My Hotel until You Are Delighted

As I keep mentioning that I'm a world traveler, I want to share with you one of my top places to stay. My favorite hotel in the world is probably the Sheraton Park Towers in Buenos Aires, Argentina, and it is not because of the marble, although there is plenty. It is because of how they make me *feel*. I liked that hotel a lot before I ran into a problem there. The problem itself wasn't that big of a deal, but the solution was nothing short of extraordinary.

In the last chapter, I said that you needed quite a few more $10 million asset employee encounters to offset even one encounter with a toxic liability, and I believe that's true. However, one extraordinary encounter with a $10M asset employee can offset quite a few encounters with toxic liabilities. This story of my encounter at the Sheraton is a case in point.

I had been waiting for room service breakfast for almost an hour. I was promised 30 minutes, and at that point I was pretty hungry and a bit irritated. Ever have that experience? What should I do? Should I call them again and ask them where it is, or wait a little bit? I decided to call. "Mr. Blue," room service said, "your order was delivered to your room 30 minutes ago."

Well, since I had been in the room the entire time, I was pretty sure she was mistaken. "No, it hasn't. I've been in the room the whole time, and no one has knocked on the door." The room service clerk promised to check it out and call me right back. About five minutes later, she called me. Sure enough, she said that the delivery person claimed he brought me my order. Now, this was getting very perplexing. Did I really need to convince them that I didn't receive the order? Can't they just take my word for it? What kind of operation were they running if they were that confused?

By then, I was getting quite irritated. Bear in mind, I really like this hotel. I stay there all the time; I have had a ton of terrific encounters there. However, at that moment, I was wondering if I liked the hotel anymore. I haven't encountered a toxic liability; I only have encountered an incompetent liability.

Kind of fickle isn't it? A ton of terrific experiences and one not-so-good one (and it wasn't even that bad), and I am considering trying another hotel. Now, mind you, I was only *thinking* about changing hotels. I would have had to reach a tipping point before I actually would switch, but that is what happens to your business every day. People tend not to remember the good experiences, and they tend to exaggerate the bad ones.

If your customers run into a few too many toxic liabilities, that will be their tipping point to switch. I wondered if I would reach the tipping point with the Sheraton on this visit. I wondered what the hotel could do to either chase me out for good, or keep me as a customer forever. At that point, I didn't think either tipping point was likely to happen, which wouldn't have been good for the Sheraton, because on my next visit I might have been inclined to try another hotel just to see what it was like. Now, I don't know about you, by I don't *ever* want a customer to try a competitor to see what it is like.

The day this happened was the second day of a five-day stay, so there was plenty of time for something to happen to make matters worse. Worse yet, there was plenty of time for nothing to happen at all and leave me wondering if I should come back the next time I was in Buenos Aires. Later in the day, I had pretty much forgotten the incident, and I went about my business. This could have been the end of the story, but it wasn't, all because of one $10 million golden asset employee that absolutely delighted me.

Her name was Anna, and she worked in guest services. Later in the day, she left a voice mail for me. As you would expect, she apologized for the incident and offered to give me a free room service meal to make up for it. Not bad, not bad at all. Lots of hotels would have let it go with an apology. Actually, lots of hotels would have let it go *without* an apology. I don't usually eat in the room, so that offer had little value to me. I called her, thanked her for her offer, and declined.

Later in the day, I received an email from her. She was not satisfied that she had done enough and wondered what she could do for me that would make up for the room service mishap. I replied, assuring her that I still loved the hotel and that she had done enough. I told her I would still give this hotel my business and that she shouldn't worry. I figured that would be the end of the story; it should have been the end of the story. In most hotels on the planet, it would have been the end of the story…but it wasn't.

You're Not Leaving My Hotel until You Are Delighted

Anna emailed me again, this time offering a free meal in one of the restaurants! She also said she hoped that would be satisfactory. Apologizing for the mishap was just not enough for Anna. Knowing she still had a satisfied customer was not good enough for her. This woman was not going to let me leave her hotel until I was absolutely delighted.

As it turns out, I was having lunch with two of my associates the next day, and we had planned to eat in one of the hotel restaurants. As a matter of fact, we had planned to eat at the most expensive restaurant in the hotel. So I told her that in an email, and she said my lunch that day would be on the hotel. Now that is pretty cool, but I was to learn soon that wasn't the end of her plan.

My associates and I had an excellent lunch that day of expensive wine and French cuisine. The total bill for the three of us had to be $500, but we never got one! We asked for the bill, and the waiter said that the meal was compliments of the hotel. I told him that there must have been some mistake. I said I knew mine was, but I didn't expect the hotel to pick up the tab for my associates.

"I am not mistaken sir," he said, "Anna was quite clear that the entire bill was to be on the house. She was very clear that you were to be delighted." I tipped him well and thanked him for his outstanding service. Later in the day, I thanked Anna. I also told her that she was a $10 million employee and encouraged her to keep up her outstanding service!

Now, I know that some of you CEO-types are sitting back and thinking, "That's ridiculous! Who authorized her to do that? Think of the cost! Oh my God, think of the

The Ten Million Dollar Employee

precedent. If we did that for every customer that had a bad experience, we would be broke!" Well, maybe if you screw up that much you deserve to be broke. Perhaps you should concentrate on the "not screwing up to begin with," and you wouldn't have to worry about giving away expensive meals.

How do you do that? You guessed it. By not having a bunch of toxic liabilities running around your business. You better hope that your $10 million employees don't need authorization to delight your most important customers, or any customers (they're all important, right?). You can make the argument that this was overkill, and maybe it was. However, one thing is for certain. This employee secured my future business—forever. This one employee removed the doubt I had about staying there again. This one employee delighted me so much that I tell anyone who will listen about my experience. It would take an act of God to tear me away from that hotel. Nothing could change my mind, except an awful encounter with that hotel's most toxic liability.

However, I am guessing the Sheraton Park Towers doesn't have any toxic liabilities. If they do, they are sure to be certain that they never meet their most important customers. I know I have never found any. In all the time I have been staying there over the course of a decade, I haven't run into even one, and trust me, I look for them! However, you don't need a bunch of toxic liabilities running around. One can do the trick very nicely. One night on an airplane, I witnessed a toxic liability destroy the future business of that airline with literally dozens of customers.

Chapter 4: All You Republicans Can Sit in Front; All You Democrats Sit in the Back

I meet some of the worst toxic liabilities on the planet on an airplane. In fact, I would venture to say that I meet toxic liabilities on every flight I take. Ever have an experience with one of them? You'd have to be living on another planet not to have suffered at least once.

I was boarding an international flight one night when I met the most toxic liability in the entire airline industry. Now, bear in mind, this chap had the distinction of being the *worst* in class. The airline world is full of toxic liabilities, but this fellow was the worst of the worst. That isn't easy to do, but he did it that night.

It was a full flight, and as is usually the case on full international flights, there was a lot of confusion among the passengers, especially the ones in coach. They hardly ever fly. They don't know where to go or what to do, and this flight was carrying mostly Brazilians who didn't speak English.

People who don't fly much depend on the flight attendants for help and guidance. For these people, the most important person on the plane is not the pilot, it is the flight attendant. Even if you are a frequent flyer, the flight attendant might as well be the CEO of the airline. They have that much power to shape the fate of the airline. Regrettably, that night on that flight, those dependent passengers had the misfortune of meeting that airline's hall-of-shame flight attendant. Let's call him "King Kong" (as this was how he acted).

I was waiting near the entrance to board the plane, along with the other business class passengers. You know how it is: When you know they are getting ready to board, you get in position so you can be one of the first to board. I knew I was in for trouble as soon as King Kong stepped off the plane to start the boarding process. He swaggered up to the business class passengers. He looked at us like we had the bubonic plague. "All of you people," he bellowed, "step away from the entrance, and don't approach until I tell you it is time to!"

Imagine him speaking to us like that. He knows we were in line for business class, so he knows who we are. He knows we pay eight times more than the coach passengers for our tickets. He knows we provide the most repeat business for the airlines. In short, he knows we are the airline's most important customers. However, he is the airline's most toxic liability, so he feels compelled to do whatever he can to destroy the value of the airline, and that night he was doing a terrific job of it.

A few minutes later, he apparently was still unsatisfied that we got the message, so he swaggered up to us again and said, "I thought I told you people to get away from the entrance! What part of this did you not understand? I will tell you when you can approach." Unbelievable. About then, I wanted to dress this guy down and demand to see his supervisor. However, I knew that would be a big mistake, because he would simply keep me off the plane and call for TSA agents. That's part of the problem with toxic flight

The Ten Million Dollar Employee

attendants: They have all the power to put you in handcuffs, and no desire to make you happy.

I took a deep breath and held my contempt for King Kong. The smart play was to simply ignore him and hope he wasn't working the business class cabin that night. Finally, His Eminence gave his approval for us to approach the entrance and we started to board. He was just inside the entrance to the plane, directing passengers to their seats. I fly so much that I knew exactly where my seat was, but I figured I better show Kong my boarding pass and let him direct me down the correct aisle. He looked at it and simply said, "You know the drill." Now that was helpful.

I settled comfortably in my seat and hoped desperately that this ignoramus was not my flight attendant. As the boarding process continued, he gave blanket directions to everyone walking onto the plane. He would simply bark, "Republicans sit in the front, Democrats sit in the back." Of course, this was a flight to South America, on which most of the passengers didn't even speak English, but he was too stupid to know that—or care.

Maybe Kong thought he was being entertaining. I found his remarks offensive, regardless of your party affiliation, and I'll bet others did, too. Of course, we business class passengers don't want to get on the wrong side of this guy, so we all kind of laughed at his stupid remarks. Nobody wanted to get in his crosshairs. Think about that for a minute. I am paying eight times the coach ticket price, and I have to be worried about getting on Kong's bad side?

Just when I thought it couldn't get worse, it did. An elderly woman was having difficulty getting down the aisle.

Republicans Can Sit in Front; Democrats Sit in the Back

She had a big bag and a few smaller ones. The bags kept banging into the seats and an occasional passenger. This woman clearly needed help to get to her seat. Do you think that's what King Kong gave her? Good guess. King Kong not only didn't help her, he humiliated her in front of all of the business class passengers. He yelled at her about how she could not go through the airplane that way, and pretty much told her to straighten up, or else. It was an awful sight to see.

I was fighting every instinct within me to slap Kong upside the head, but I knew where that would get me. I got up and started helping this woman out as best as I could. In the meantime, Kong looked at the woman, shook his head, and said, "Folks, I can't make this kind of stupidity up. Really, I don't make this stuff up." Maybe Kong thought his next job was on Leno. One thing's for sure, he needs a next job.

The next day I sent an email to the airline's customer service group detailing the incident. I am a VIP on this airline, so I knew I could get someone's attention. After an investigation, you won't believe what they told me. "Thank you for your feedback, Mr. Blue. We have had concerns about this employee before (ya think?), and we plan to send him for some sensitivity training."

Send King Kong to sensitivity training? Are you kidding me? He needs to be sent to the bone yard for boneheads! He needs to be canned, fired, terminated, discharged, dumped! Take the grievance, go to arbitration if you have to, but lose this loser!!!! It's not bad enough he treated this poor woman so badly. She needed help, not humiliation. It's not bad enough that half the plane witnessed his toxic behavior. It's not bad enough that he treated the business class customers like idiots. That's all bad, but it isn't the worst part.

King Kong isn't the only one who should be shipped off to Siberia. His supervisor should be canned, too. He has to know that Kong is toxic as all get-out, and he should be fired for letting this guy get away with it. I know what you are thinking: Maybe he was just having a bad day. I doubt it, but I would suggest the most powerful people on an airline can't be allowed to have bad days. Would you care if your neurosurgeon was having a bad day?

Think about this another way: Imagine you are on a small regional jet flying into small airport on a snowy, turbulent December evening. Cups and baggage are flying everywhere. On top of that, the visibility is near zero. The flight attendants have been ordered to sit down because of the potential danger of the impending landing. At that moment, you are wondering if you have enough life insurance. You have two pilots up front. One of them is the best in class, an "A" player. He had the best grades in flight school, the best proficiency check-ride scores, and the best record in the airline. The other pilot scraped by with a "C." His proficiency scores were not so good, but they were good enough to get by. Your problem tonight is that the C pilot is landing the airplane, not the A guy, and he is having a bad day. I don't know; let's send him to sensitivity training—if you survive the landing.

I'll bet you think that's not a good analogy. I'll bet you're thinking that it's one thing if a pilot flies a plane into the ground, killing all the passengers and destroying the aircraft. What Kong is doing is quite another thing—fairly harmless, but irritating at worst. However, King Kong is destroying the brand and the future of the airline as surely as if he were flying that plane into the ground. It will just take him a little longer. He destroys the airline one day at a time, on every flight of every week of every month, through every year, and they want to send him to sensitivity training?

That's not the scary part. How many other King Kongs does this airline have running around? Multiply that number by the number of toxic encounters they all have with that airline's most important customers, and the airline is doomed. If I were the CEO of this airline, this would scare the hell out of me, and I would do something about it right away. However, most won't, and do you know why? Well, I am not exactly sure, but I have a few theories. They will blame union agreements, that's for sure. Who negotiated those agreements? They will blame a tedious and protracted disciplinary process that seldom yields satisfactory results—so they shouldn't try?

The real problem is this: These CEOs live for the financial balance sheet. They minimize liabilities and maximize assets. They don't understand—or don't accept—that the employee balance sheet is the problem. They don't accept that the toxic liabilities on the employee balance sheet are destroying their company.

Don't misunderstand me; I live for the financial balance sheet, too. We CEOs live and die by the financial balance sheet. However, you already know that the financial balance sheet is a result of the operations of the company. Good operations produce a good financial balance sheet, and bad operations produce a bad one. You need to understand

The Ten Million Dollar Employee

that the employee balance sheet is the most important tool you have to produce a good financial balance sheet. In fact, I would go so far as to say that it is the *only* tool you have. Ignore it at your peril.

Republicans Can Sit in Front; Democrats Sit in the Back

Chapter 5: Lessons from a Hole in the Wall in South America

I often have pondered what makes the difference between a toxic liability and a $10 million asset. I am confounded when I find employees that work at the same company, for the same boss, under the same working conditions, but act vastly different.

I was once at a dumpy restaurant in South America. This was a small smoke-filled *cantina* with bad food and worse service, the kind of place where the cockroaches are complimentary. This place looked like a scene from the Antonio Banderas movie *Once Upon a Time in Mexico*. You know the scene I mean, where Cheech Marin was the bartender?

Now, the waiters there were not very motivated, to say the least. I can't say that I blame them. They were treated poorly and probably made a dollar a day if they were lucky. Their lives were simple, and they weren't about to let me complicate them. Punch the clock, deliver the slop, and go home for a *cerveza* and watch a soccer game. There was no reason for any of them to care, but one did.

As I expected, I was having a hard time getting my order taken. Most of them just ignored me. Now, I can get myself through a fundamental conversation in Spanish, but I was getting nowhere.

Lessons from a Hole in the Wall in South America

All I wanted was a coffee, but that seemed to be more than this restaurant's toxic liabilities could muster. I was just about ready to give up and pay the bill, when a waiter came up to me and in broken English said, "Can I help you, sir?" Now, right from the get-go, I was impressed that he made the attempt to speak to me in my own language. Why would he do that? After all, I wasn't in Kansas, Toto.

His name was Ricardo. I asked him where he learned English. He told me he lived in Boston for a time. Then I asked him why he spoke to me in English. He told me he knew I would be more comfortable if he did, and that he might *serve me better*. Now, that was very impressive. I was in a dive restaurant where every single employee but one could care less, but this one wants to *serve me better*! Well, he has pretty much figured I am an American, and the likelihood of him seeing me again is near zero. However, he wants me to have a positive impression of the restaurant!

Have you ever had that experience with a hotel, or an airline? You can be at the same hotel, or on the same flight, and have two very different experiences from two very different employees. Why is that?

I am not sure I will ever know the answer to that question, but I do know this: As a CEO, I can't control the attitudes of my employees, I can only influence them with a culture that supports the $10M asset employee. However, I can control whether employees work for me or not. I submit to you that wasting time trying to rehabilitate toxic employees is a fool's errand. It can't be done. Therefore, my job is simple, but not easy: Root out the toxic liability employees and replace them with $10 million asset employees. Dump the toxic ones and elevate the asset ones to hero status in the company. It is the CEO's most important job to see to it that this is done.

However, let's return to my *cantina* story. My somewhat-English-speaking waiter delivered my coffee very quickly. The last thing he said was, "Please let me know if I can do anything else for you, sir." This guy is working at a place where nobody cares. His boss doesn't care. The owner doesn't care. The customers are used to bad service, and they probably don't care either, but he cares. This guy isn't going to make any more money if he delights one customer in a room full of customers that don't care. This guy isn't going to get kudos from his boss because he made one *gringo* happy. His efforts probably will go unnoticed, and yet, he insists on delivering the best service he can, in spite of all of that. Every day, he fights the good fight. Every day, he faces his toxic opponents and builds value for his company. He is a hero in a world of toxic adversaries, and he is losing the battle.

This is going on in your company right now. At this moment, a battle is raging over the future of your company. It's not between you and your competition. It's not a battle between the forces of the market and your new product developments. It is not the battle of the brands, it is the battle of the employee balance sheets. It is between your most toxic liabilities and your $10M assets, and your $10M assets are probably losing.

Why? There is no doubt in my mind that it is because you have too many of the toxic types to offset the assets. Remember, one toxic liability can cancel out dozens of customer encounters with $10M assets, if not all of them. Let me tell you a story about how one toxic liability is costing a furniture store millions.

I have been buying furniture from the same furniture store for nearly 13 years. I'll bet I have spent over $30K with this store if I have spent a dime. Until my toxic encounter, I had planned on spending a lot more. Now, $30K should get their attention, when the average value of a normal customer over the same period is probably a quarter of that. For the longest time, I was very satisfied with the way I was treated there. Notice that I said "the way I was treated," and not another factor, such as how well I liked the furniture, the quality, etc. Remember, your best customers care most about how they are treated; everything else is secondary.

The last purchase I made there became my final purchase because I met their most toxic liability after the furniture was delivered. These were two very expensive recliners, and they didn't work right from day one. They would suddenly start reclining without warning; it was like a gear kept slipping or something. They wouldn't go back all the way, just enough to make you think that the whole thing would fall apart.

I called the store, and they sent Mr. Toxic-Head (the service manager) out to my house to find out what was wrong. He wasn't a very pleasant sort of fellow, but at first he only appeared to be toxic-neutral. It was clear he didn't enjoy being around people in general, and customers in particular. You have to figure they keep a guy like this in the warehouse for a reason.

Mr. Toxic-Head examined the recliners and explained to me that there wasn't anything wrong with them. It was true that the defect sometimes appeared and sometimes not, which I explained to him. He persisted in declaring that there wasn't anything wrong with them and left.

At this point, I was not too happy. He wasn't exactly calling me a liar, but he wasn't exactly not calling me a liar. Considering that I was one of their most important customers, if he couldn't find the problem, he should have given me two new recliners. However, that would be too much work for him. He would have to argue with the manufacturer, fill out a bunch of paperwork, and get them to exchange the chairs. I guess he figured my next $30K with the store wasn't worth all of that.

Unfortunately, the story gets worse. A few weeks later, I mostly had forgotten about the incident, but my 15-year old daughter (who just had leg surgery and was on crutches at the time) had not. I had bought these recliners for her exclusive use in the room in which she spends most of her time, but she refused to sit on them because she was afraid they would collapse and injure her. Minor annoyances in life become major problems when your 15-year old daughter is not happy, so I called the store again. I explained that after all the money I had spent there, now I had two recliners that my 15-year-old daughter, who was on crutches, was afraid to sit on for fear of their collapse. I explained that since I had bought them exclusively for her, they were useless to me.

Oh, what a bother, Mr. Toxic-Head thought. He came to the house again and reluctantly adjusted the reclining mechanism. He told me that he didn't believe there was really anything wrong (there he goes again, not exactly calling me a liar, but not exactly not calling me a liar), but he would adjust them anyway. By now, he didn't like me very much, and I really didn't like him. This is the guy they choose to meet their most important customer.

That was the point where Mr. Toxic-Head was in the deep end of the pool and should have been calling for a lifeguard. He should have alerted his boss that a VIP was not happy and he couldn't make him happy. However, he didn't, because Mr. Toxic-Head didn't care about making me happy. Your most toxic liabilities don't either. By then, I was probably not going to buy anything else from that company ever again, and something that happened shortly after sealed that decision.

I was sitting on one of the recliners one night. As I started getting out of it, the whole thing tipped over and collapsed to the floor, with me on it! I was furious, as I could only imagine what would have happened if it had collapsed on my daughter while she was recovering from surgery.

The next day I marched into the store, convinced that they must take the chairs back and give me a full refund. I explained what happened to Mr. Toxic-Head. He explained to me how in all of his vast experience, he was quite certain that what I described was impossible. Well, at least he was finally calling me a liar. To make matters worse, he never even once asked me if I was injured in the fall! Things got pretty heated when the store manager refused to take the recliners back for a refund. She said that the store policy prohibited refunds. I told her I wanted to talk to the owner, only to be told, "The owner doesn't talk to customers!" That's swift. Heaven forbid the owner should talk to his most important customer.

The Ten Million Dollar Employee

However, talk to me he did, but only after I launched a formal complaint with the corporate franchise CEO. Only then did the owner personally inspect the recliners, with a service manager from one of his other stores (I had warned him that I didn't want to ever see Mr. Toxic-Head again). When I advised him, CEO to CEO, about Mr. Toxic-Head's behavior, he did admit that yes, they had some concerns about him, and that they were working on his interpersonal skills. Sounds like sending King Kong to charm school to me. I see this all the time. I've said it before: *Someone* knows who your toxic liabilities are and they choose not to do anything about it. In this case, the owner knew, and he should be fired for not doing anything about it. Who can fire the owner? I can, and I did. I never did business with him again. What's worse is that I told everyone I know what happened. Their first response? "I won't buy my furniture there!"

However, why don't they just remove Mr. Toxic-Head? I've been around a long time, and I can tell you it would be for one of five reasons:

1.   He's been around a long time.

Your customers don't care how long he has been around. Your customers only care about what is happening to them *right now*. I didn't care about all the positive experiences I had with this company over the years. I only cared about the moment I met Mr. Toxic-Head, not how long he had been around.

Lessons from a Hole in the Wall in South America

2.   We can't pay that position enough to get a $10M asset.

How about spending a little less on marble and chandeliers, and investing that money in $10M asset employees? I could make the case that spending more on this position creates value for the company, or at the very least, avoids losing value in the future. Let's do the math: Assume a conservative estimate that Mr. Toxic-Head drives 100 of your most important customers away a year. Let's assume that those 100 customers spend $10K per year. Over the course of 10 years, that business loses $10M! Still think they can't pay that position enough?

3.   Some human resource weenie says there isn't enough documentation, also known as, "The union won't let me."

Human resource weenies will always say there isn't enough documentation, and most labor lawyers will say the same thing (not mine, by the way, I don't hire weenies). If you insist on taking their counsel, make them tell you exactly how much is enough, and then go build your case. Unions won't ever let you fire an employee. Their job is to keep employees, especially the toxic ones, not to fire them. Toxic employees depend upon the union for protection and will always vote for them. Besides, who's running your business, you or the union (ok that's a trick question, in many cases it *is* the unions)?

4.   His boss is afraid of confrontation.

This is a very common reason. Mr. Toxic-Head probably intimidates his boss. The job of every manager in your company is not to make the widgets, or sell the widgets. The job of every manager in your company should be to create a culture that weeds out toxicity and promotes $10M assets. If the boss can't take the heat, it's time to get him out of the kitchen.

5.   He's shown signs of improvement lately. Let's give him another chance.

I used to say that attitude always catches up to you. It does, unless you have numbers 3 and 4 going against you. Toxic types only show improvement when the heat rises. Don't misunderstand me, everyone deserves a second chance if they make a mistake. However, no one deserves a second chance with a bad attitude. Believe me when I tell you that I have tried to turn around bad attitudes. It has never worked, not even once.

Returning to my story, the owner ended up replacing the internal mechanism, but still refused to refund my money and take the recliners back. He said that it would set a dangerous precedent with other customers. Well, I don't care about his precedent problems, but the point is this: Why should it be a dangerous precedent to satisfy your best customer? Why was he worried about replacing his product if he believes in it to begin with? How about making sure that the product is right, and then you don't have to worry about a dangerous precedent being set because you had to replace a product that wasn't right from the start? Only toxic liabilities all the way down the line could have produced a product that wasn't right from the start.

This is typical when management is more concerned with giving toxic employees second chances than they are about losing their best customers. This case also is a bit unusual because the owner/CEO is himself a toxic liability. Want to know where those recliners are now? In an empty room where no one uses them; I think I'll give them to charity. Maybe the owner of the furniture store can use them when his toxic liabilities destroy his business.

Speaking of toxic liabilities, these days the teaching industry comes in for a lot of criticism, in some cases deservedly so. I used to believe that, until I met "Mr. G."

Chapter 6: We're Not Teachers, We're Character Builders

I doubt you would argue that the impact a teacher can have on a young mind can last a lifetime. It can be a positive or negative impact. Unfortunately, many times teachers have no impact on young minds at all. That is because many of them show up for work and simply spit out the lesson plan. Even worse, some of them teach toxic attitudes about society.

You can find $10M toxic teachers all over the place. There are the ones who don't care, or the ones who are tenured and don't need to care. It is unusual to find a $10M asset teacher. An extraordinary example of this is Dave Gudmastad, affectionately called "Mr. G" by his students.

Mr. G is a music teacher and band director at Cotter High School in Winona, Minnesota, and his job is very difficult. Every year, he receives new freshman students and has to integrate them into the marching band. While that may sound simple, this is an award-winning band. Every year, they compete against other bands, many of them from larger schools with more resources, and every year they take first or second place in almost every competition.

Mr. G is a true $10M asset and a leader in every sense of the word. He has to forge all these young people into a cohesive, commanding, and effective team, and every year, 25% of his team turns over! Now that's tough. However, Mr. G is not teaching them how to march, nor is he teaching them how to play an instrument. He is not teaching them how to win awards. Winning awards, in my view, is secondary. He is teaching them something far more important. He teaches them respect: respect for the team, respect for each other, and respect for themselves. Once, when some of the band members were not treating others properly, Mr. G got right into that and had a discussion with them about respect.

He teaches them discipline. You wouldn't believe the tight formation these kids have in competition. As an example, when they are marching backwards, they all march on their *toes*. I saw them once at a performance in Chicago. It was a long time between bands, so all the bands had to wait awhile in the queuing area before they could step off. The other waiting band members were sort of milling around. Many of them were fussy and just sort of hung out in loose formation, but not Mr. G's band. Mr. G's band was in tight formation, perfectly still, like wooden soldiers. There was none of that sloppy hanging around for them. Now that's discipline.

He teaches them hard work and commitment. I once had a discussion with my son, who was in the band at the time, and I said, "Steve, Mr. G works you guys pretty hard. How do you feel about that?" He simply said, "Dad, that's why we win." Wow, what a neural connection! These kids are learning to be future $10M asset employees. Not only that, Mr. G is teaching these kids to be $10M people! Mr. G's students will be successful, wonderful contributors to the world, no matter what they decide to do with their lives, and all because Mr. G decided he wasn't in the band-building business. He decided he was in the character-building

The Ten Million Dollar Employee

business. This is all because Mr. G decided years ago to be a $10M asset himself.

Winning awards is not Mr. G's business. Winning awards is only the tool he uses to build future $10M people. This is the type of manager you want in your business, managers who are in the business of building $10M employees.

Terry Greene is a marketing/sales instructor at Minnesota State College Southeast Technical. Just like Mr. G, somewhere along the line, Terry decided he wouldn't simply come to work each day and simply deliver a sales/marketing curriculum. Somewhere along the line, Terry decided his job was much more important than that. Somewhere along the line, Terry decided to be a $10M asset. Not just to the school, but a $10M asset to the students. He recently won the Teacher of the Week award. His students nominated him, and this quote from one of them pretty much summarizes him well: "Terry always goes above and beyond for his students and the people he works with. He's always there to help, not only for his students, but anyone at the school. He makes each and every class enjoyable and worth going to. I've never met a teacher who cares more about the success of his students."

Nor have I. My son, Steven, is one of those students, and Terry is making an enormous impact in his life. He always seems to know what's going on with Steven. He has a vested interest in Steven being successful, not just in the classroom, but in life. If the quote above is any indication, he doesn't play favorites. He invests his life in making all his kids successful. He doesn't just punch the clock, deliver the lecture, and then go home. He is truly a $10M asset. Terry is in the business of producing $10M people, and thank God he is not the only teacher doing the same thing.

Gabe Manrique is a $10M economics professor at Winona State University, and the past dean of the business school. Gabe's a pretty smart guy. He holds a PhD in Economics from the University of Notre Dame, but that's not his greatest strength. His greatest strength is the impact he makes on his students. Not just by lecturing, but by giving them $10M real-world learning experiences in some of the most unusual places.

Gabe has led his students in study-abroad programs in London, Turkey, Egypt, Brazil, and the Phillipines. This is not easy duty. Imagine leading a bunch of kids, who are barely out of high school, to a third-world country!

I was privileged to co-chair one of his travel-study programs to Brazil. Gabe and I (mostly Gabe) gave them years of exposure to Brazil in seven days. We provided them with in-depth experience in almost every part of Brazilian life: culture, education, politics, and business. I facilitated the business side by exposing them to a real-world business situation of a U.S.-Brazilian joint venture, but Gabe worked a lot harder at it than me.

He and his wife Cecilia (who is also a professor and works at the University of Wisconsin) planned every detail of the trip with exacting precision. He didn't want the students to have an experience. He wanted them to have a $10M experience, and he did that and more.

The group arrived at about 9 A.M. on the first morning. They went from one activity to another until 5 A.M. the next morning. He had them up three hours later to take in

The Ten Million Dollar Employee

some cultural activities. As Gabe said, "They can sleep when they get home."

He packed in everything he possibly could in the short time we had. Even after we arrived, he was trying to find more experiences for them. He obsessed over making this the most powerful experience in their lives, and he succeeded. Now, this is not the work of someone who is only going through the motions of teaching. This is the work of a $10M teacher, and one who is shaping future $10M people.

In Gabe's own words, "In moments of conceit, I suppose I can allow myself to think that perhaps one of them will be inspired to travel more, to be more inquisitive about the world and to be more understanding of others. And I can hope that some of the stories that I tell every semester—for indeed teaching involves a lot of storytelling—will inspire students to learn meaningful things about some things, whatever those may be." I think he is being modest. He inspires his students to be better than they think they can be. This one $10M teacher is raising a whole generation of $10M people, and guess what? Someday they will be your $10M employees.

Luke Merchlewitz gets kids long before they get into Gabe's hands. Luke is an elementary teacher who absolutely loves his job, and his kids. You can see it in Luke's face when he is around the kids. His face absolutely beams. Luke was chosen as a top-ten finalist for the National Education Association's Award for Teacher Excellence. The whole community knows Luke is an exceptional teacher and constantly works for the betterment of the community. His commitment to his students was also recognized in 2009 when he received the Winona Teacher of the Year award. That same year he was named a finalist for the Minnesota Teacher of the Year Award.

Luke once said, "Not only must an entire school do what is best for its children, but the entire community must participate as well. Together and united, we must show our children how responsible, conscientious and respectful citizens act." Now that is the thinking of a $10M teacher! Luke works tirelessly not only to educate his students, but to teach them how to be responsible and important contributors to the future of our world. He could do what many teachers do: walk in, go through the lesson plan, and then go home, but he doesn't. He is not a teacher. He is a character builder. Somewhere along the line, Luke chose to be a $10 million asset.

Is that where it all starts? Does the $10M employee start with Mr. G, Terry Greene, Luke Merchelwitz, or Gabe Manrique? Perhaps it does. I know in Gabe's case that his early $10M shaping was from one of his first college professors. He told me about this professor: "From the first day of class, I was enthralled by his storytelling. His class periods were so engaging that it did not seem that one was attending lectures. I was awed by his knowledge and ability to communicate. That class, and others like it, inspired me to pursue a career accumulating and disseminating knowledge."

When you are in a hotel, why does one maid take extra care and line up all of your toiletries in the bathroom, but another does not? At Walmart, why does one checkout employee do her job with a smile, when another does not (yes, I have witnessed smiling Walmart checkout

The Ten Million Dollar Employee

employees)? Why did that South American waiter go the extra mile with me when the others could care less? Somehow, the $10M asset employees must have been shaped by $10M people.

Clearly, our teachers are shaping a whole world of $10M people. However, we want them shaping assets, not liabilities. That is one of the reasons I invest heavily in supporting the educational system in my community, and you should, too. However, we can't know what the early shaping has been with our employees. In some cases, psychological testing will reveal that, but that process is usually not performed on the rank and file.

One thing I know for sure: Once you get a disgruntled $10M toxic liability, it is way too late to do anything about him. He has already had a lifetime of shaping to become so toxic. Toxic shaping may have started with his parents, or with his teachers. Certainly, some of his toxic shaping came from working for toxic supervisors.

You shouldn't try to re-shape toxic liabilities. The only thing you can do is remove them from your balance sheet, every single one of them, and then replace them with $10M assets. Sound like a tall order? It is. However, it's not impossible if you commit yourself to it.

Chapter 7: Restructuring the Employee Balance Sheet

I wish I could tell you this is something you can delegate to the human delight people (human resources). Actually, I don't wish I could tell you that; it is not. In fact, that is the worst place to delegate this. Human resource people are all about making people happy. Happy people are not necessarily $10M assets. They are not necessarily more productive than unhappy people; they are just...well...happy. You are not in the happy business.

You are in the business of creating a cadre of $10M superheroes. A cadre that is so strong, so customer focused, and so jazzed up that your competition can't come close, one that "won't let you leave my hotel until I can delight you." You want a cadre that won't let the students come home until they have had a life-altering experience. A cadre that insists on giving you the best experience they can possibly give you, even though they know you'll never come back.

That's your only sustainable advantage in the coming global business apocalypse. Make no mistake, the apocalypse is coming, whether you are ready for it or not. Your cool new products won't save you. Your cool new capital equipment won't save you. Your cool new alliances or code-sharing agreements won't save you. All these things can't save you, but Valter Castro can.

Valter Castro is an unassuming man in his mid-fifties. He is very cultured and polite, a gentleman's gentleman.

Restructuring the Employee Balance Sheet

Valter lives with his wife near Copacabana Beach in Rio de Janeiro, Brazil. Like many Brazilians, Valter is happy if he can have a beer and spend time with his family. Valter is a good father and husband. He raised a fine son, Ricardo, who is one of the youngest precinct captains in the Rio de Janeiro Police. He adores his granddaughter. However, unlike some Brazilians (and many employees), Valter is a $10M asset, and it's not just because he saved my life one day.

Valter and I got caught once in the middle of a gunfight between the federal police and drug runners from one of Rio de Janeiro's *favelas* (drug slums). Valter was driving the car as we traveled on a busy eight-lane highway in an industrial section of the city. I wasn't paying much attention, when traffic came to a screeching halt and I heard what sounded like a tire blowing out, and then I thought I heard firecrackers. One thing I have learned since that day is that if you think you hear firecrackers in a third-world country—think gunfire instead, automatic gunfire.

I looked up from my book expecting to see a big traffic jam, but to my surprise, all the traffic in front of us had cleared away. I thought that was kind of odd, until the killing started. A federal police officer, complete with flak jacket and automatic weapon, was chasing a guy across this eight-lane highway. When he got close enough, he shot the guy dead, right in front of us…and then he turned toward us.

I was terrified. I heard more gunfire. The cop that just killed a guy is wildly motioning us toward him—toward all the gunfire? Toward the shoot-out? That's when Valter shouted, "Get down!"

The Ten Million Dollar Employee

Valter speaks three languages. His native tongue is Portuguese, but he also speaks English and French fluently. When Valter speaks in English, you can hardly detect that it is not his first language. He taught himself these languages while he was a diamond sales representative on some of the largest cruise ships in the world.

Valter traveled the world as a diamond salesman. In that role, he met people from all countries and all cultures. The years he spent doing this honed Valter into quite the worldly, sophisticated gentleman, and after that, Valter could have done anything. He tried to start his own business, but it just didn't work out. It hardly ever does in Brazil, where it is almost impossible for the average guy to do that.

After his diamond selling days came to an end, Valter went to work for a tour and travel company in Rio as a driver. With all his sophistication and intelligence, this is the work he chose to do, and he chose to do it as a $10M asset employee. In the middle of that gunfight, Valter really was earning his pay. His very life was in danger (well, so was mine, come to think of it) that day, and we both wondered if we were going to survive the encounter.

Mind you, the company Valter works for, Diplomat Services, has nothing but good people. I have done business with them for years, and have yet to find a toxic liability. However, that is not the same thing as finding a $10M asset. Not finding anything bad doesn't leave lasting impressions on you, while $10M assets do. This is why it is not enough for your company to have no toxic liabilities. The absence of toxic liabilities won't distinguish you in the marketplace. The absence of toxic liabilities won't save you in the global trenches of business. You need to do more than that.

You need to have a bunch of Valters running around. Aside from saving my life that day (which you would think would put him in the $10M asset hall of fame), Valter is the most perfect driver on the face of the planet. You can think of wanting anything and Valter will have it for you. Don't even try and step out of the car with even a hint of a drizzle—he will be right there with the umbrella.

One time, I didn't think I would need him, so I told him he could have the night off. Later that evening, I called him and asked if he could come around and pick me up so I could have some dinner. He responded that he couldn't, because earlier he had a beer. After all, who can blame him? I gave him the night off. I told him not to worry about it and called room service instead of going out.

The next day, he was apologizing all over the place. He said, "Mr. Blue, I am very sorry I was not available to you last night. I should not have had that beer, just in case you changed your mind. I am embarrassed this happened, and I want you to know that will *never* happen again."

Trust me when I tell you that I tried to assure Valter that it was OK; I tried to assure him that he wasn't at fault because I changed my mind. He was having none of it. He continued to insist he acted badly and that it would never happen again.

Here's a pop quiz. How many toxic liabilities does it take to lose a customer? I don't know. However, I do know this. It would take a bunch of toxic liabilities from Diplomat Services before they could offset the goodwill Valter has built with me. If your company has even one $10M Valter, it would take quite a quite a few toxic liability encounters before you would start losing customers.

Now, don't misunderstand me. I am not giving you a flyer on having toxic liabilities; you can't afford any. I am just trying to illustrate the point that you need the $10M superheroes to offset the toxic liabilities you do have, because as hard as you try, you will always have some toxic liabilities lying in the weeds. Think of employees like Valter as your weed killer!

You have to re-shape your employee balance sheet to eliminate toxic liabilities and elevate your $10M assets to hero status. That sounds like an easy thing to do, but it is not. Your organization will give you a million reasons why it is not necessary, or even possible.

Restructuring the Employee Balance Sheet

Chapter 8: Case Studies in Toxic Turnarounds

I once thought one of my greatest achievements as a CEO would be to turn a toxic liability into a golden asset. After all, as the CEO, I have the power to do most things that affect how an employee feels about the company and the customer. I can change whatever conditions existed before me that created their toxicity.

Never one to take an easy challenge, I decided to start with the most toxic employee in the company. I decided I would either change him into a golden asset, or ask him to leave the company. This guy was a particularly tough nut. He was the head of the labor union, and a crusty guy with a bad attitude. He hated his job. He hated his co-workers. He hated the company, and he hated me. Even though he hardly knew me (I had just joined the company at the time), he decided he would be my worst nightmare. Little did he know, my worst nightmare was a lot worse than he could ever be.

As the head of the union, it was his job to block everything management wanted to do, and he was good at it. I couldn't even think about doing something without him slapping us with a grievance. As any good union guy would, he'd slap one right on top of the other. I needed to make a substantial change in this company, and I needed him to be on board with it. He didn't want to be on board with anything. All he wanted to do was sit around (he did very little work) and file grievances.

Case Studies in Toxic Turnarounds

He had the dream job of a $10M toxic liability: sitting around doing nothing, whiling away the hours complaining to anyone who would listen. Every now and again, he would block and tackle anyone who had the audacity to try and make things better. In fact, this guy was the archetypical toxic employee. He could wreck a…Well, let's just say he was the perfect candidate to try my grand experiment. I would turn him around, and then write a book about it!

When I walked into his office, Bernie (name changed to protect the guilty) was doing what he usually did: nothing. He was somewhat surprised that I would casually walk into his office and strike up a conversation. My predecessor never did that. Actually, my predecessor referred to employees as "bodies." Why would you want to strike up a conversation with a "body?"

Bernie looked at me the way you might eyeball a mortal enemy. In his mind, that is what I was. He was conditioned over decades to hate "the man." He was conditioned over decades to hate this company. "Hi Bernie," I said, "How are you? Mind if I sit down?" He grunted something about the CEO being able to sit anywhere he wanted, and offered no inkling that this would remotely resemble a civil conversation.

"Bernie, I know the way this company has treated its employees in the past has not been correct. I don't believe in treating our employees poorly. I believe employees are valued partners in the business and should be treated as such. Now, I don't expect you to believe my words. They're just words. I intend to back the words up with actions. But I need your help."

The Ten Million Dollar Employee

He was twisting in his chair uncomfortably. He didn't believe a word of it, and he knew he couldn't have that conversation with me and still be a good union steward. He was conflicted, and he was having difficulty processing the conversation.

"You'll get no help from me." He was spitting his words out, practically choking on each one. I thought he was going to throw up. He screwed up his bearded face into a little ball of fur (he did that from time to time) and hammered the other nail in: "It is not my job to help you. It is my job to look out for the employees."

Fair enough. That's what unions are supposed to do. However, where is it written in stone that the interests of employees and the company can't be aligned? I will concede that in some cases they are not. In some cases, the company doesn't deserve an aligned workforce, because management is a bunch of boneheads. However, I was determined to align the interests of the employees and the company.

When I first took over this company, they weren't aligned. Employees were treated as depreciating assets. Actually, they were treated as depreciating liabilities. No wonder they consequently acted like depreciating and toxic liabilities! I guarantee that if you treat your employees like liabilities, they will act that way. It's not their fault; it's yours. I was determined to change all that. I improved wages and benefits. I changed out most of the management team and replaced them with managers who treated people like assets. However, I still needed to get Bernie on my side to make any real progress. I still had this notion I could take the company's most toxic asset and turn him into a $10M employee.

Case Studies in Toxic Turnarounds

I offered to take him on a business trip to see one of our most important suppliers, which was something he had never done before. He was to get on an airplane and spend a few days away from the company on business. This was the supplier that provided the raw materials that Bernie worked with every day. He was astounded that I would do that. I still remember what he said when I asked him if he wanted to go with me. He asked me, "Is that possible?"

I figured if I got him out to see the world around us, he might have a different perspective. I thought that if I could get this guy away from the office and spend some time with him, he might see my point of view. I assumed that if I treated him like an asset, instead of a liability, I could change his perspective—and his attitude. It worked for a while. About that time, I was fancying myself an enlightened CEO. I had this formula down, baby! I was the renaissance CEO, bringing about major cultural change one toxic liability at a time.

I couldn't have been more wrong. He could not get over his hatred for the company. Mind you, by this time, the "company" wasn't anything like it used to be. I had changed most of its management. I had improved wages and benefits. I took a personal interest in him and tried to bring him in the fold, but he couldn't escape his DNA. He couldn't escape his decades of programming. He couldn't escape whatever influences in his life caused him to hate the company, *any* company, forever, so I fired him.

Ever the optimist, I wasn't about to give up on changing toxics to goldens. After all, I was the CEO, and if I couldn't make major attitude shifts in my company, then who could? I focused my efforts on an equally challenging, but perhaps easier to convert employee. Let's call him Tom.

Tom was a toxic's toxic. However, he was especially toxic because he fancied himself a clever guy. Do you know the type I mean? He has it all figured out, and you don't. He pontificates about the problems of the company and he knows how to fix them. Interestingly, he feels no need to tell you how. He doesn't want to solve any of the problems, because if he did, he would have nothing to pontificate about, and then he would lose the power he has over the unwashed and unholy masses. Those were the other employees who looked to Tom to fuel their continuing discontent.

Tom was a very hard case. When I first arrived at the company, I would occasionally walk by his area in the factory and say hello. One thing I found curious was that he had a big sign in his area with the number 96 posted on it. A few days later the number was 94. I really didn't think much of it, dismissing it as a countdown to a special occasion or something.

Not long after, someone clued me in to what the special occasion was. My predecessor only had lasted about 100 days on the job (I know the average tenure of a CEO is not long, but come on, 100 days?). Tom was keeping a scorecard, for the entire company to see, as to how long I would last as their CEO! Now that's toxic!

Imagine how I felt when I found out. I just moved my family into town. Took my young children out of their comfort zone and into a place where they had to make all new friends. I had built a brand-new expensive house, and put my career on the line in a high-risk move hoping that this new

Case Studies in Toxic Turnarounds

CEO gig would work out. I knew that the guy before me had only lasted several months.

It was irritating (not to mention unprofessional) that Tom, arguably the company's second most toxic liability, was making a game out of when I might get canned. He proudly was displaying the Doomsday Clock of my career. What was worse was that he figured he could do so with impunity. Needless to say, I was furious. When I found out, I marched straight out to confront him about it.

"Tom," I said. "What's that sign all about?" He took a deep breath and said, "Well, that's a little hard to explain." "I'll bet it is. I'm a good listener, why don't you give me a shot?" At that point, he lamely explained what the sign meant, and tried to put the best lipstick he could on this pig.

I honestly think he believed that no one would tell me what the sign meant. Unfortunately, he mostly was correct, which gives you a hint as to the toxicity of the employee balance sheet when I arrived at that company. I dressed him down pretty good for the sign and made him take it down. However, I didn't fire him, because I had it in my head that I could turn this toxic liability into a golden asset. I couldn't have been more wrong.

I began taking a personal interest in Tom. I asked my team what his problem was and what the company did to create it. Over the course of several months, I corrected his legitimate issues (and he had a few) one-by-one. Every time I went into the factory, I would chat with him to see where his head was.

I asked him to serve on several ad hoc "how do we fix this" committees. I gave him tons of respect and treated him as a valued asset. I even put him on an acquisition integration team when we bought a competitor. For a while, he showed real promise. For a while, I began to believe I had the formula down for transforming a toxic liability into an asset. I started believing that my failure with Bernie was a fluke, an unusual and unique case of a "toxic gone wild," or a toxic gone too far to bring back from the brink.

I was wrong. Tom, like every other toxic liability I have ever met, couldn't make the transition to a golden asset. He couldn't even make the transition to not being quite so toxic. You know what? He *didn't want to*. After all those years of sniping at the company, he couldn't turn back. His whole self-image was wrapped around being the company critic, and he couldn't change that. He didn't want to change that. He even deluded himself into thinking the other employees didn't want him to change. He believed that they needed him to be the company critic, the great pontificator with all the wisdom. He enjoyed playing the role of the wise one who called into question everything the company did.

I should have fired him the first time I had the chance. True to my belief that your attitude always catches up to you, his did. He finally did a few galactically stupid things (*ya think?*) and was extremely insubordinate to his boss, so I fired him. I didn't worry about preserving his dignity when I did it. I did it loudly and publicly so the other toxics would get the message.

So what's the message here? I cannot convert a toxic liability into a golden asset. I can't even neutralize a toxic liability, and *neither can you*. Therefore, you shouldn't try. You can only get rid of the toxic liabilities, and the faster you do so, the better. Don't waste any time attempting to convert them. Instead, focus your efforts on the golden assets, and if you must, the fence-sitters.

The fence-sitters are a special case. They don't exactly hate the company, but they don't love it either. They are spectators in the game, but they aren't playing it. They watch the battle between the toxics and the goldens with interest. They don't have any particular stake in the outcome, but what fun and sport it is to watch the game!

I am a pretty simple guy, with pretty simple views, so you will conclude my prescription for the fence-sitters is, well…simple. It is. You need to have about one conversation with them that goes like this: "If you want to stay in this company, you have a decision to make, and you have to make it right now. We are committed to having an all-star team, all of whom are $10 million assets. Every single employee in this company will either be a $10M asset or they will be gone. There is no room for fence-sitters and spectators in this game. You decide what you want to be, and tomorrow I will either have your commitment to being a $10M asset, or I will have your resignation."

You should offer to help the fence-sitters make the transition. If they have the right attitude, they deserve to be helped along. Additionally, you need to be certain that you are running the kind of company that has earned the right to have $10M asset employees. Assuming you have done that, give the fence-sitters a short leash to make the change, and cut them loose if they can't. After all, how long does your customer give you to get your act together?

Chapter 9: The Eternal Battle between the Toxics and the Goldens

When I fly, because I am in the top tier of the airline's most frequent flyers, I get treated very well, but only by a part of the airline. The airline created a special customer care unit for people like me, and they treat me like a king. Unfortunately, other parts of the airline (read: some flight attendants) treat me like a donkey. Mind you, this is the same airline that is treating me like royalty and a horse's ass all in the same day! In spite of the fact that everyone in contact with me knows that I am a VIP, I don't get treated like a VIP by everyone.

The airline knows this. It knows it has toxic gorillas running around, and so it attempts to offset them with a special customer care unit. Then it hopes the customer care unit can undo the damage done by the King Kongs.

The airline has put nothing but $10M assets in this special unit. They are golden assets. These people really get it. They are the best of the best, and they treat me exceedingly well. How well do they treat me? Recently, I had a very tight connection coming into the country, and this entire team was literally *running* down the concourse to make sure my flight didn't leave until I got there. They know me by name and ask how my children (by name) are doing. If there is even a hint of flight delays, they back me up on another flight without my even asking. They sweep me through customs at the front of the pilot's line. I don't have to show my lounge club card to enter; they take care of that. I don't walk between gates, they give me a ride. The people in this unit are absolutely superb and delightful.

If any team of golden assets could offset the toxic idiots that the airline has, this team could do it, but it can't. As good as this team is, they are not enough to undo the damage done by people at the same airline who treat me like the hind end of an animal. In fact, the very same day this superb team escorted me to the gate is when I met King Kong (remember him?). He proceeded to wreck that entire superb team's efforts.

It's a shame, because in this particular case, the $10M golden assets are losing the battle to the $10M toxic liabilities. This is happening in your company right now. Your $10M golden assets are valiantly fighting a losing battle against your most toxic liabilities, and it's not their fault, it's yours. You'll lose your golden asset employees to your competition. Eventually, you will lose the global war of business, and you'll lose your job, and you'll deserve it.

You see, some companies take what they think is the easy way out, or more likely, they are taking what they see as the *only* way out. As they can't (or won't) take out the toxics, they try and offset them with other assets: Bose headsets, moist cookies at the front desk, or a special unit to take care of the best customers. They wouldn't need to do most of this if they would simply deal with the fundamental problem and eliminate all the toxic liabilities.

The lesson is that there is no substitute for cleaning up your employee balance sheet. Adding special units and moist cookies won't save your company. Sending King Kong to charm school (Faye Wray would have appreciated that) won't save your company. Offering special incentives and discounts (shudder at the thought!) won't save your company. The only thing that will save your company is to invite your toxic liabilities to work for your competitors.

It's extremely important to be certain your entire company is aligned behind your $10M golden assets. It won't work if any of the toxic liabilities are allowed to stay on the staff. First of all, the toxics will try and poison the goldens. They have to, because misery loves company. Second, the toxics will undo all the good the goldens do with your customers. That's what toxics do.

However, it doesn't have to be that way. Some companies make sure they don't have even one toxic liability, and I find them in the most unlikely places. An example of this is the Custom Alarm Company in Winona, Minnesota.

Alarm companies are notorious for having bad customer service. I don't have to name names. You know what I mean. Most of them pledge terrific response to alarms and half the time their employees are half-asleep when you need them.

Not so with Custom Alarm. In a decade of doing business with this company, I have yet to find even one toxic employee. Over the years, we have had quite a number of times that we have inadvertently set off a false alarm. Every single time, within minutes, a Custom employee will call to find out if everything is alright. They have never failed to do this, not even once. Every time they have called (invariably knowing it may be a false alarm), the employee on the other end of the call was extremely courteous and professional, every single time. They never complain that I am setting off too many false alarms. They never seem put out that they have to call and confirm that I have done something stupid (yet again). Every single employee I ever have had contact with simply does their job cheerily and professionally. Is that the kind of company you want? You know it is.

I find $10 million golden employees in even more unlikely places. When is the last time you were really happy with a plumbing contractor? OK, maybe you have never been happy with a plumbing contractor. On the whole, they charge too much, take too long to get to your house, and aren't a very customer friendly bunch.

This is not the case with H&M Plumbing in Rollingstone, Minnesota. I have done business with them for nearly 13 years. Just like Custom Alarm, they are in the kind of business where it would be easy not to bother distinguishing themselves from the competition. They could take the attitude that since the rest of the pack is bad, why should they work hard to be better?

However, they do. Each and every employee at H&M is a $10 million golden asset. Each and every encounter I ever have had with this company, in 13 years, has been very positive. They provide fast, friendly service at a reasonable price. Believe me, if anybody can have a bad day, it would have to be a plumbing contractor. However, if their employees ever have had a bad day, they certainly have concealed it from me. How does this work? How is it that employees in a pretty dirty business never even have one bad day? Well, I am not certain, but I do know this: It starts with

The Ten Million Dollar Employee

the CEO. The CEO of H&M made a commitment that his employees would never have a bad day. He only hires and keeps $10 million golden assets. If he ever had a toxic liability, he must have gotten rid of him fast, because I have never found him.

Let's contrast H&M with my water softening company (actually, my ex-water softening company). I have done business with this company for over 30 years. One day, their most toxic liability wrecked that 30 years of goodwill in one telephone call. I was supposed to have the large heavy bags of water softener delivered right to the softener in the basement, but one day they stopped doing it. I called to find out why. She could not have cared less, and it showed.

She didn't see her job as nurturing a VIP. She saw her job as getting me off the phone as quickly as possible so she could go back to the "real work" (whatever she saw that as). She treated me coldly and impersonally. What I wanted to hear was, "I'll fix that problem right away for you, sir." What I got was, "I'll pass along your complaint to somebody." To make a short story shorter, she either never passed it along, or other toxic liabilities figured it wasn't important enough to solve. After a while of not hearing anything, I just dropped them, after 30 years, and no one even bothered to call me to ask why. Do you suppose this is happening in your company? I know it is.

The Eternal Battle between the Toxics and the Goldens

Chapter 10: You Deserve the Company You Create

This is a two-sided issue. On the one side, I ask you, as the CEO, the following: What kind of company do you want to run? Do you want to run a company with a bunch of toxics running around destroying your brand, or do you want to run a company with a bunch of golden asset superheroes running around destroying your competition? Do you want an army of King Kongs in your company, or do you want a legion of Valter Castros? Which force is more likely to win the coming global apacolypse? Which force is more likely to advance your company in the marketplace? Which force is more likely to decimate your competition? Which force is more likely to decimate your company?

These may sound like trick questions. What CEO in his right mind would pick the toxic option? Why would any CEO want a company where everyone hates the company? Why would a CEO choose the option of employing people that hate the customers? Why would any CEO choose to run a company with such a toxic environment that it literally can make people sick?

However, it happens all the time. The CEOs pick the toxic option either by default or design. I know this to be true, because I run into "King Kong" everywhere. I run into "Bernie" and "Tom" almost every day. Just the other day, I ran into a waiter that never should be allowed near a customer, but he was, and the most important touch point for a restaurant customer is the waiter. Even if the food is terrific, a toxic waiter can ruin the whole dining experience. On the other hand, if the food is not so good, a golden asset waiter can give you a reason to consider coming back again.

Mr. Toxic-Wait did not fall into the latter category. This guy was very abrupt and rude with me when I asked for a drink. He mumbled something about how I must be blind or stupid not to see he had a lot of other customers to take care of, and would get to me when—and if—he could. Mind you, he didn't apologize for the delay. He didn't make me feel special (remember what I said about the most important thing is how a customer *feels*?). Oh, but he did make me feel something, alright: He made me feel like taking my business elsewhere.

I told Mr. Toxic-Wait that he should be ashamed of himself for speaking to a customer that way (remember, I am the guy who writes books about this, so I can't simply ignore a toxic when I see one). I asked him how in the Dickens he ever got a job on the front line of the customer touch point? By then, he was looking at me like I was from another planet. He was not used to customers pushing back at him at all, much less questioning his qualifications for his job.

I now know I can't turn a toxic, especially not one that doesn't work for me, so I was not expecting much. Not surprisingly, he just sort of sneered at me and went along his merry way ignoring me. That's fine. There are lots of restaurants in the world. I don't need this one. Your customers have lots of options in the world, too; they don't need your company. Don't forget that.

The Ten Million Dollar Employee

This is my point about CEOs choosing to run toxic companies. Somebody has to know this waiter is toxic, and yet they have chosen to put him on the front line of the business. They have chosen to place him at the most important touch point of the restaurant. In short, they have chosen to place their most toxic liability where he can meet their most important customers. Who knows how many other people he repelled that day? How many other people does he repel every day? How much does the restaurant lose in repeat business because of this guy? How much does your business lose in repeat business because of your toxic liabilities?

"But good help is hard to find," you say, especially in the hospitality business. That may be true, but a guy like him should be working in the kitchen on dishes, not in the dining room on customers. If you think you can't afford a golden asset in the dining room, do the math. Assume that this guy chases away two customers a day, six days a week, 52 weeks a year. Add up their tabs, and you'll find it is a pretty big number. You'd be better off paying a guy like this to stay home.

Therefore, I know for a fact that as improbable as it seems, many CEOs are running toxic companies. Quite simply, they either know it or they don't know it. There is no middle ground here. If they know it, they should be fired for not fixing it. If they don't know it, they should be fired for not knowing it. Too simplistic, you say? I don't think so, but more on that later.

For now, let's look at the other side of this two-sided issue: the employee side. What kind of company do your employees want you to run? Do they want you to run a toxic company or a company with golden superheroes? What kind of company do your employees want to work for, a "toxic sludge-in-the-wall," or a "shining company on the hill?" This may sound like a trick question, but the answer is anything but obvious.

I once took over a company that was so toxic, I could almost see it in the air. As soon as I walked into the place, I could *feel* the toxicity. This is not hard to spot if you know the signs. The tempo of a company is either upbeat or it's not (there I go, being simplistic again). As soon as you walk into the place, you'll either feel it or you won't.

When I walk into a company, I always feel *something*. I either feel an atmosphere of collaboration and a certain buzz of high energy, or I feel a blanket of suppression and anxiety—or hostility. I could walk into your company tomorrow, and within one hour I could tell you what your employee balance sheet looks like. I could predict your current and future earnings (remember Carnac the Magnificent?).

I knew as soon as I walked into this company that I would have my hands full changing its future. More to the point, after spending one hour in this company, I knew I would have my hands full *saving* its future. This may be the problem confronting your company today. Your problem may not be in shaping the future; your problem may be that you're in danger of not having a future at all.

Most employees in this company hated the management. Well, truth be told, they had good reason to, which is something I fixed quickly. Most employees also hated the customers. Well, truth be told, that is never OK, no matter what. Perhaps most telling and worst of all, most employees hated each other. They refused to sit in the cafeteria at the same time. They often shouted obscenities at each other. They wouldn't talk to each other (except for swearing of course) unless absolutely necessary, and then the conversations were short and brittle.

Whenever I walked into the factory, it felt like walking into a funeral home. It was a lot like going to a wake. Like a wake, no one was happy to be there. Like a wake, no one spoke unless necessary, and like a wake, everyone couldn't wait to get the heck out of there. Sounds like a great place to work, no? Now, do you think this kind of environment had an impact on the earnings of the company?

In this particular case, the earnings of the company were pretty good, so the management team was quite smug about not needing any enlightened "hold hands and sing Kumbaya" philosophies. They figured the right kind of employee was a toxic employee. They figured (correctly so) that toxic employees would be the cheapest to employ and not be the swiftest bunch on the boat. They didn't see any reason to have thinking people when "bodies" (how they referred to the employees) would do. Bodies don't talk back, or even think. Bodies simply do what they are told, while the "smart guys" make all the decisions.

As the earnings were pretty good, they couldn't imagine how they could be better. Therefore, they didn't see any sense in investing any time, money, or effort into changing the toxicity of the place when all they needed was themselves—the smart guys that were already running the place. Let me tell you, these guys had a serious case of narcissistic personality disorder!

I don't know about you, but I won't ever work in a toxic environment again. I say "ever again," because I have worked in such places, although never as CEO. The last toxic environment I worked in was so bad that going to work would literally turn my stomach. I couldn't sleep at night because of the horrible days I had, and the days weren't horrible because of complex, challenging problems, or difficult customers. The days were horrible because the place was horribly toxic, and it was the CEO's fault (here's a hint: It's always the CEO's fault).

The CEO treated his managers in a demanding, demeaning manner. Therefore, his managers treated their employees in a demanding, demeaning manner. Therefore, the employees treated the customers in a demanding, demeaning manner. Therefore…You get the picture.

The place was highly political. In executive meetings, everyone had to be on their guard to protect themselves from an ambush from one of their colleagues. The point of these meetings wasn't meaningful dialogue to find solutions and move the business ahead. Heaven forbid, that's not why toxic sludge pools are made. The point of these meetings was to make the other guy look bad, so as to divert attention away from whatever you weren't doing right.

These tended to be marathon meetings. We would start at 7 A.M. and often not finish until well after 10 P.M., and then we would start over again the very next morning. They were brutal, with a great deal of yelling and accusations. There were massive amounts of "Why in the hell did you do

The Ten Million Dollar Employee

this?" going around, in addition to "Why in the hell didn't you do this?" and the CEO condoned this. Sometimes, he even encouraged it. He had some twisted notion that competition among his executives would somehow drive better performance. While to a certain extent healthy competition does drive performance, toxic competition only drives more toxicity, and ultimately lower performance (or even no performance).

It's not hard to see that the apple doesn't fall far from the tree. The executives would leave these toxic slug-fests feeling, well…toxic. When you are in that kind of sludge, day in and day out, it wears you down, and it is nearly impossible not to become toxic yourself. After a while, toxic seems to feel normal. The executives would leave these meetings and then they would treat their employees the same way they were just treated. Toxic waste does flow downhill.

While we were in the meetings, our employees were trying to figure out who was getting the best of whom during the meeting. It was almost like they were watching gladiators fight, and the conference room was the Coliseum. The whole company was more concerned about which executive won that day's contest then they were about earnings and customers, and the executives were preoccupied with having all the weapons they needed to win that day's contest. Moving the business ahead was not on the agenda; survival was.

Have you ever worked for a company like that? If you've been around for a while, I bet you have. Unfortunately, I believe that many companies in America today are a lot like that one, to one degree or another. It's a wonder they aren't all out of business.

You Deserve the Company You Create

Who would want to work under those conditions? Only two types of people: toxics, who like being in a toxic environment (yes, they do exist), or people who can't find another job. What's worse for you as a CEO is that you are probably paying these toxics so much that they can't afford to leave. I would call this a self-inflicted wound. You get what you pay for. Therefore, when you are running a company like that, all you have to run it with are people that nobody else wants: the toxics and the ones that can't get another job because they aren't worth much. That's a great way to boost earnings, no?

Let us return to my story. "Bernie" and "Tom" (and a host of other failed attempts) have taught me not to try and change toxics into goldens. Therefore, when I took over the toxic company with the pretty good earnings, my course was clear. I had to eliminate every single toxic employee. Every single one of them, and I did, although it took a number of years. This is not an easy process, and needs to be mapped out and executed carefully. However, it needs to be done if you want to be the shining company on the hill. The results will be at the end of the rainbow.

In this particular case, not long after all the toxics had been removed, earnings had doubled, and employee productivity skyrocketed. I didn't need the smart guys that were running the place to do it; I just needed an entire company of $10M superheroes. There I go again, being simplistic. As a matter of fact, I asked the smart guys to leave. I know I can't turn toxics around (or narcissists either), so I didn't waste any time trying to rehabilitate them.

Chapter 11: Should You Be Fired?

Remember I said in the last chapter that if you are a CEO and you are running a toxic company, you either know it or you don't? I also said that if you know it and aren't fixing it, you should be fired, and if you don't know you're running a toxic company, you should be fired. This is the chapter where you have to fess up and take a long, hard look at yourself and your company. This is the part where you either decide to be a super-CEO, or a dud looking for a job; you decide.

Are you running a toxic company and you know it? Maybe you didn't know it before you read this book, but now you do. Well, good for you. That's why you read this book to begin with, and if this book gave you a wake-up call and you are ready to take action, bravo! However, if you are running a toxic company and you don't know it even after reading this book, you're in real trouble.

Most CEOs make the mistake of delegating human resources issues to the "health and happiness" department. That's a big mistake. The worst place to leave the problem of your toxic liabilities is with people who are in the business of making employees happy. The health and happiness department will never support an agenda as controversial as this. They won't understand it, and they will resist it all the way.

Should You Be Fired?

This is too important to leave it in the hands of amateurs. Would you trust your happiness department to restructure your balance sheet? Of course not, and you shouldn't trust them to restructure your employee balance sheet, either. This will be a very foreign concept to them.

The only role you want them to play is to outplace the toxic liabilities you will lose in the process. Just be wary in the event that they try and undermine your program (happiness people have been known to do this). Make it clear to them that if they aren't 110% in agreement with this, they will be the first ones to go. Then you need to follow up with them to make sure they aren't just giving you lip service (happiness people do that).

This has to be *your* program, and it should be. You are embarking on a quest that is nothing less than fundamentally changing your entire company. If you screw it up, you won't have a company. You have to take a personal interest in this. You have to be committed 110% to the $10 million golden asset concept. You have to be its chief architect, cheerleader, and battalion commander. Make no mistake, when you do this, you will be going into battle against all the toxic liabilities in your company, and there is no guarantee that you will win.

It will be difficult and messy. It will be frustrating and scary. At times, you will wonder whether the ticket was worth the ride, so you better strap on your flak jacket before you start. This will be the toughest thing you have ever done, but you won't be alone. Others have gone before you, and some of them had a much tougher time than you ever will—like my friend and business partner, Roberto Rocha.

The Ten Million Dollar Employee

Roberto is the CEO of CMBA, a company in Brazil. Roberto has a very tough job. He and his partners successfully completed a leveraged buyout (LBO) of the company in 2005. This is not an easy thing to do in a country like Brazil. The cost of capital is quite high, as much as 30-35% a year, and governmental regulation of business is complicated and extensive. While labor is plentiful and cheap, the quality on the whole is not that good. The odds of a regular guy like Roberto being successful in Brazil are quite low. However, he has not only done it, he has prospered.

His company has grown extensively since the LBO. Not only has he expanded in Brazil, he has taken major market shares from his competition around the world. He has increased profit, lowered costs, improved quality, and provided a consistent stream of dividends to his shareholders along the way. Roberto has been a success, despite the odds, because of his personal philosophies about the kind of company he wants to run. Roberto has beaten the odds because he is a $10 million golden asset, and he demands the same from everyone in his company.

Roberto likes to say, "I can only do my best," and that is the philosophy he employs throughout his entire business. He works tirelessly and expects all of his employees to do their best, as well. He is the indefatigable optimist. One time I took him to play golf in the United States. He had never done it before, and he could barely hit the ball five feet. Before long, he actually hit it about 10 feet, and he was ecstatic! He said, "See, I have already improved 100%!" It is this eternal optimism and his philosophy of improvement that has made him and his company so successful. These may seem like simple concepts, and they are, but they translate into expecting nothing but $10 million golden assets in his workforce.

Roberto doesn't mess around with the also-rans. He doesn't tolerate toxic liabilities, he just loses them. He settles for nothing less than a total strike force of $10 million assets. If he can do it in a less-developed country, you can certainly do it here.

Don't assume you are not running a toxic company. Assume you are until you can get proof to the contrary. I think it is a pretty safe bet that most CEOs are running toxic companies. This has to be true, or I wouldn't keep running into them every time I go anywhere.

So, what do you do? Where do you start? Well, you have to start by making a major declaration and policy statement. You have to declare that you will no longer tolerate any toxic employees in your company from this day forward, *period.*

Bold statement, isn't it? Your human resources people and your lawyers will give you a million reasons as to why you can't back up that statement. Your senior managers will give you the second million reasons why you can't do that. Actually, the first thing they will do is try and convince you that the problem doesn't exist. Don't you believe it! It does; I guarantee it.

There will be certain managers on your team who won't buy into this. In some cases, it will be because they are toxic liabilities themselves. It may be because they have allowed these toxic liabilities to exist for years, and don't think they can do anything about it now. These managers have to be the first to go. Anyone who doesn't go along with this can't stay on the bus. Invite them to work for your competition.

You always can change the terms of engagement with your employees. You simply have to make the declaration. It goes something like this: "I know we have tolerated a certain behavior from some of our employees for a long time. That was yesterday. Starting tomorrow, that behavior will no longer be tolerated. Anyone who doesn't want to go along with the new program can't stay" (there I go again, being simplistic). As soon as you make your "no more toxics" declaration, you have to start inviting people to work for your competition right away. You must be ready to start the firings before you make the declaration. Certainly, it will take some planning. You need to start recruiting in advance to make sure the work gets done when the toxics depart. However, you will probably find you don't even need to replace some of the toxics, because they weren't doing any work other than, well…being toxic.

Of course, it is more complicated when you have labor agreements in place. However, you can re-negotiate them the next time around to be more management-friendly (remember the management rights clause?). Perhaps you think you can't. If you think that, you are doomed. You have the contract that *you* negotiated. Don't blame the union for something to which you agreed. Change it the next time around.

You have to articulate very clearly the new behaviors that are expected. You have to give your employees a little time to change their behavior, but not much time. Remember, you can't change a toxic into a golden, you can only get rid of them; therefore, don't even try. The only crowd you have half a chance with is your fence-sitters. Spend a little time trying to convert them, but not much. Remember, your $10 million golden asset competitors aren't sitting around waiting for you to clean up your act.

You have to start with your executive team and roll this out one layer at a time. You can't have toxics below you and ask them to eliminate toxics below them. Get the first layer below you taken care of first. If you get the right $10 million employees on your executive team, then it's time for them to do the same thing with the layer below them. Then that layer takes care of the next. Before you know it, you will have an entire company of $10 million golden super-assets.

Now you know. Now you can see what I see every day: toxic liabilities and golden assets, battling every day for the future of every company in the world, including yours. Consider this: If most of the business world is losing the battle to the toxics (and I believe that they are), just imagine what will happen to your earnings once you've re-tooled your employee balance sheet. Your company will be unstoppable!

Now that you know, you have no excuse not to take the right action to transform your company to a legion of superheroes. If you don't, you have no one to blame but yourself, and you deserve to be fired. Just imagine how much better the world would be if every CEO took my advice and re-tooled their companies into $10 million golden assets? Imagine being delighted by the airlines. Imagine calling a plumber anywhere and getting fast, friendly service at an affordable price. Imagine never running into another rude waiter again. Imagine how competitive the United States would be against China if it had nothing but $10 million super-heroes in its companies. We could destroy them!

As a CEO, you have a responsibility to your company to do this. You have a responsibility to your shareholders. You have a responsibility to the $10 million golden employees you have that get sick thinking about work because of all the toxicity you haven't eliminated. You also have a responsibility to your country; it needs you to accomplish this so the good old US of A doesn't become a less-developed country in the future. I know this can be done. I have seen it done in companies large and small. I have done it in companies large and small, and so can you. Good luck!

Should You Be Fired?

Acclaim for Burnarounds: Unlocking The Double Digit Profit Code

Steve's first book, *Burnarounds: Unlocking The Double Digit Profit Code* has become the field guide for CEO's who want to dramatically increase profit.

Burnarounds explains that many American companies are slowly trudging along with a sense of entitlement and complacence. They are satisfied with "business as usual", and rarely make thorough investigations into decreased productivity, latent R&D, underperforming salespeople, or an outdated factory. The bleak reality of this situation is that many CEOs and company heads cannot detect the severity of these problems until it is far too late; they are deciding whether or not to pay their electric bill, or trying to find the least painful route for bankruptcy declaration. *Burnarounds*, through the powerful and expert teachings of Mr. Steve Blue, offers the opportunity for these companies to do a 180 and blaze a trail towards immense profits and prosperity.

What readers have said about *Burnarounds*:

Steve Blue shows how to value time as a currency equal to money, with zero tolerance for mediocrity in people and performance. I've seen him walk the talk in quickly lopping off those who refuse to get with the program, but celebrating those who do, with the results showing up in the financial statements. You can follow his simple (but not easy) lessons, if you have the courage.

Norm Stoehr
Founder, Inner Circle International, Ltd.

Steve Blue provides a framework to maximize firm efficiency in a global economy. He promotes an aggressive approach to whip underperforming companies into shape. His straightforward, no-nonsense blueprint provides an easy-to-follow guide to transforming an organization by addressing hard issues that many companies would rather avoid.

Dr. Greg Filbeck, CFA, FRM, CAIA
Professor of Finance
Penn State Behrend

Burnarounds is much more than a cookbook—it's a blueprint for supercharging your sleeping giant of a company into an organization that is profitable *and* a great place to work for all. I recommend this book for any leader with guts enough to stage their own burnaround (you'll never regret it!).

James D. Kestenbaum, Ph.D.
The Solutions Group

To order your copy, go to www.stevebluewebsite.com, or www.amazon.com

www.ingramcontent.com/pod-product-compliance
Lightning Source LLC
Chambersburg PA
CBHW060622200326
41521CB00007B/852

9 7 8 0 9 8 2 2 5 8 9 0 3